The Imaginative Explorer's Guide to the Library

Eric Braun

BLACK
RABBIT
BOOKS

Hi Jinx is published by Black Rabbit Books
P.O. Box 3263, Mankato, Minnesota, 56002.
www.blackrabbitbooks.com
Copyright © 2021 Black Rabbit Books

Marysa Storm, editor; Michael Sellner, designer;
Omay Ayres, photo researcher

Names: Braun, Eric, 1971- author.
Title: The imaginative explorer's guide to the library / Eric Braun.
Description: Mankato, Minnesota : Black Rabbit Books, [2021]
Series: Hi Jinx. The imaginative explorer's guide
Includes bibliographical references. | Audience: Ages 8-12.
Audience: Grades 4-6.
Summary: "Invites readers to take a fresh, creative look at the
library through playful, conversational text and fun tips"–
Provided by publisher.
Identifiers: LCCN 2019026828 (print) | LCCN 2019026829 (ebook)
ISBN 9781623103286 (hardcover) | ISBN 9781644664247 (paperback)
ISBN 9781623104221 (adobe pdf)
Subjects: LCSH: Libraries–Juvenile literature.
Classification: LCC Z665.5 .B73 2021 (print) | LCC Z665.5 (ebook)
DDC 027-dc23
LC record available at
https://lccn.loc.gov/2019026828
LC ebook record available at
https://lccn.loc.gov/2019026829

Printed in the United States. 1/20

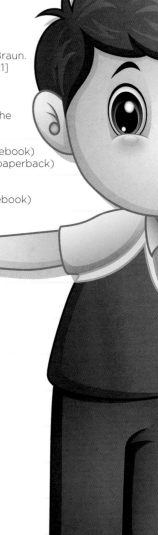

Image Credits

Alamy: BNP Design Studio, Cover; Cidepix, Cover, 15; Ingram
Publishing, 18–19; Dreamstime: Segoviadesign, 11; Suryadi
Djasman Kartodiwiryo, 2–3; Tetiana Morgunova, 12–13; iStock:
Dualororua, 6–7; Memo Angeles, 4; Shutterstock: Alena Kozlova,
4–5; anfisa focusova, 16; ekler, 17; GraphicsRF, 8, 16, 23;
larryrains, Cover, 14–15, 15; Lorelyn Medina, 21; Lukiyanova
Natalia frenta, 19; mark stay, 6–7; mejnak, 4; Memo Angeles, 1,
5, 12, 12–13, 16, 18, 18–19, 19, 20; mhatzapa, 9; mohinimurti,
3, 15, 21; opicobello, 14; Pasko Maksim, 7, 13, 23, 24; ONYXprj,
Cover, 14–15; pitju, 5, 21; Reginast777, 15; ridjam, 11; Ron Dale,
6, 7, 9, 10, 13, 14, 17, 20; Ron Leishman, 16; TheToonCompany.
com, Cover, 15; Tyler Olson, 20; Verzzh, 16; Victor Brave, Cover,
15; Every effort has been made to contact copyright holders for
material reproduced in this book. Any omissions will be rectified
in subsequent printings if notice is given to the publisher.

Contents

Chapter 1

Too Much Information

Oh, Em, Gee! You are, like, so totally bored. You took 200 selfies. You texted all your friends. You told them every single move you made. But then they stopped texting back. Maybe it's time to find something else to do.

Check It Out!

Why not take your imagination to the library? The library is a world of books and information. It's also a world of endless adventure. You just need to explore it!

Chapter 2

Sharing Smiles

Spreading some happiness is a great way to spend the afternoon. And the library is a great place to do it! Just bring some slips of paper to the library. Write nice notes on them. They can say things like, "Have an AWESOME day!" or "You're better than French fries." Once you have your notes, stick them in popular books. People will be happy to find them.

Miming

You can also get people smiling by miming. Miming is when you pretend to do something without making any noise. It's a lot like **charades**. You could silently bounce an invisible basketball. Or fly a kite. Or rescue a kitten from a giant dragon with three heads and five tails! See what gets the biggest **reaction**.

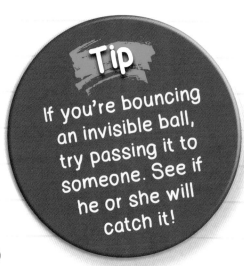

Tip

If you're bouncing an invisible ball, try passing it to someone. See if he or she will catch it!

Chapter 3

Brilliant Books

Books are magical. They can take you to new worlds and tell you fun facts. They can help you get people laughing too. Just head to the library's cookbook section. Find a delicious recipe to **recite** to a parent or librarian. How-to books work well for this too! Maybe your dad would like to hear a **dramatic** reading of how to **fly-fish**.

Tip

To recite something, you need to put feeling in your voice. Change your speaking speed and volume.

Judging a Book by Its Cover

The library is a great place for some healthy competition! Challenge a friend or parent to find the book with the cutest cover. (If you're brave, you can try finding the grossest or scariest cover instead.) Set a timer for five minutes, and get searching. When time is up, show off your books and pick a winner. Have a librarian break any ties.

Tip

Make sure you put the books on re-shelving carts when you're done. Or check them out!

Chapter 4

Fun Faces

Libraries are full of amazing books. They're also home to an incredible tool … the copy machine! Bring in **headshots** of your friends. Then use the machine to make copies of them. Once you have copies, cut out parts from different faces. Grab an eye from one person and another from someone else. Choose a different forehead, hair, and chin. Glue the parts together into a brand-new face.

Tip

Copies aren't free. Make sure you bring some money to the library.

Keep an Eye Out!

Funny faces make good posters too. Make a MISSING or WANTED poster for your **collage**. Or make a poster for a popular book character. Draw a character on a sheet of paper. Write "MISSING" or "WANTED" at the top. Add a description of the character below your picture. Offer a silly reward for any information, and post it to a bulletin board.

There's a lot of exploring to do at the library. All you need is a little imagination.

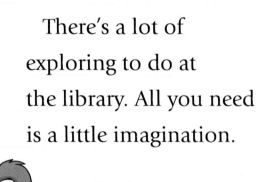

Chapter 5

Get in on the Hi Jinx

If you liked exploring the library, you might want to become a librarian someday. Librarians help people find books to read and organize reading programs. Librarians also use their imaginations to bring stories to life for young visitors. Maybe someday you'll be a librarian. Until then, keep exploring the library!

Take It One Step More

1. **Why are libraries important?**

2. **Invent your own wacky library. What sort of things can people check out there?**

3. **Do you think you'd like a job as a librarian? Why or why not?**

GLOSSARY

charades (shuh-REYDZ)—a game in which some of the players try to guess a word or phrase from the actions of another player who may not speak

collage (kuh-LAHZH)—a work of art made by gluing pieces of different materials to a flat surface

dramatic (druh-MAT-ik)—attracting attention

fly-fish (FLAHY-fish)—the activity of catching fish by using artificial flies

headshot (HED-shot)—a photograph of a person's head and face

reaction (ree-AK-shun)—the way someone acts or feels in response to something that happens

recite (ri-SAHYT)—to read something out loud

BOOKS

Devos, Sarah. *I Am Never Bored: The Best Ever Craft and Activity Book for Kids: 100 Great Ideas for Kids to Do When There Is Nothing to Do.* Beverly, MA: Quarry Books, an imprint of The Quarto Group, 2018.

Holzweiss, Kristina A. *Amazing Makerspace DIY Movers.* A True Book. New York: Children's Press, 2018.

Peterson, Megan Cooley. *Pranks to Play around Town.* Humorous Hi Jinx. Mankato, MN: Black Rabbit Books, 2018.

WEBSITES

Library Facts for Kids
kids.kiddle.co/Library

For Kids | Education & Careers
ala.org/educationcareers/
libcareers/kids

INDEX

B

book covers, 14

C

copy machines, 17

L

leaving notes, 9

librarians, 13, 14, 20

M

miming, 10

P

posters, 18

R

reciting writing, 13